Walking the Ridge Line

Peter.
Chistmas 2016
Many thanks
for all your help
+ support.

Roz

Walking the Ridge Line

Robin Moss

First published 2015
by Mudfog Press
c/o Arts and Events, Culture and Tourism,
P.O. Box 99A, Civic Centre, Middlesbrough, TS1 2QQ
www.mudfog.co.uk

Cover Design by turnbull.fineart@btinternet.com

Print by Evoprint & Design Ltd.

ISBN: 978-1-8995039-8-8

Mudfog Press gratefully acknowledges
the support of Arts Council England.

For Jean, Kate and Rebecca

With thanks to all the members of the Bridge Writing Group in Newcastle who first saw many of these poems, and especial thanks to Ellen Phethean for her mentoring skills and patience.

"Does writing make it Truth?"
Ellen Phethean

Contents

Voyager

That journey,
every day passing his mates travelling
in the opposite direction,
ignoring their studied aversions of gaze,
the up yours salutes,
his cap flung over the garden hedge;

that journey,
made from a house with no books,
with only
the Mirror and News of the World to read,
where music was a noise -
but Love, ill-afforded extra tuition
and the Eleven-Plus, gave him the ticket
for the trip to this page,

like the spacecraft Voyager
flung into interstellar space,
hijacking gravity to swing by Jupiter to Saturn, onto Neptune,
achieving escape velocity as he passed
into the heliosphere of words, their music,
moving from Yeats to Lawrence, to Hughes,
onto Plath and Heaney and beyond,
powered by the solar wind of reading and language,
losing his Suffolk accent on the way,

trying not to forget what he still called home,
rereading *The Making of The English Working Class*,
looking back
on the fading,
tiny green planet
of his
past.

Rattled

'an enchanted land'

On the Sellotaped cover of your first-ever book,
a man clings to a liana, sloth-style,
crossing the river,
leg over leg,
hand over hand,
gun slung over his shoulder,
watched anxiously by Martin,
that group of brown-skinned Indians on the far bank,
and you -
your mind's eye page-hooked,
hoping he'd make it safely to the other side.

'more and more astonishing'

The creeping jungle, its sinister shadows of green,
the sun-shocked yellow banks of an azure-blue torrent,
those dangerous red flowers –
how exotic and strange it all was,
this unimagined world
you were entering,
word by magic word.

'the voyage'

Inscribed
'for good work, highest on points 1955-56',
your Mum and Dad bought you *Carib Gold,*
Treasure Island, Marooned on Mars,
David Copperfield, all those stories of escape,
the perils and joys of journeys, hand over hand,
to reach what waits on the far side of reading.

'Martin reflects much and forms a firm resolve'

Here they all are, shelved,
cherished
like poppy seed-pods
held to the ear,
seeds inside
rattled.

Ticker

He sat on guard outside his front door,
shins always gaitered up,
whiskered jowels overhanging
the unstudded shirt, waistcoat strung with the coiled chain
of a pocket-buffed fob watch;

he'd doze, wake, take it out, open up the case,
stare at time as if he believed it had stopped,
put it to his ear to listen,
while we shouted *tic toc, tic toc Ticker* as we passed.

Or the ball we were kicking
would hammer his window pane,
and he'd start up, eyes whited out, gargling and gasping,
clutching at his face for the mask he'd never found,
his breath a wounded bellows,
then the rachitic cough
rattling him for minutes until he'd hoicked up
something raw and green
from half-gone lungs,
a yellow fog
lurking still.

He'd shout, shake his fist,
take out the watch, check the time,
his other enemy,
days
all gas and gaiters.

Lost and Found

'Greenwood was not, then, like Dante's selva oscura the darkling
forest where one lost oneself at the entrance to hell. It was
something like the exact opposite: the place where one found
oneself.' Simon Schama – *Landscape and Memory*

1

All that green swallowed you whole.
There were no signs,
no large carved wooden fingers pointing the way out,

just trees
an infinity of forest, (was it Epping?)
when you got lost aged seven,

the game of hiding,
till you were nowhere,
running on and on,

paths that came and went,
forked into choices
you couldn't make,

seeing only shadows,
the faces they imagined up
chased by voices from riddles and rhymes,

cloven-footed creatures
coming to gobble you down, bone by bone,
no warm hand to hold, to guide you back to love.

Then, an end to trees,
a cricket match, blue sky, the ringing of bells,
cups of tea and hugs.

2

Isn't it strange
your life's affinity with forests and trees?
How safe you feel

lost in the imagination of leaves, branches,
their whispering shade
and tangled roots,

emerging into sudden light,
that echo hidden within you, running in circles
around love, being found,

now hand in hand
with your children's children,
walking the woods, loved again.

Sex in the 1950s

Saturday morning haircuts perched on a board
set across the barber's chair,
men gawping at copies of Parade,
poring over revelations of breasts
they tried not to let you see,
waiting for the furtive question, eye-brows raised,
anything for the weekend? –
What did it all mean?
As strange as the mysteries of why girls wore knickers
and didn't have your bits.

That divorced woman, who lived in the houses at the back
your mother declared *she wouldn't be seen dead with,*
always at the pub, *her kids outside till all hours*
stuffing their faces with pokes of chips or crisps,
(of whom you were jealous, but didn't dare say),
her sat inside with her *latest fancy piece,* drinking gins and orange,
no shame at *giving it away.*

Colin from next door, the *Nancy boy* with the funny voice,
seen holding hands with his friend in the next street
 - no harm in him -
but never trusted, you never knew why,
to take you and your sister to school.

Those days of going steady, popping the question,
the village hall wedding do and beer in crates,
all the gossip about the girl down the road
in the family way, after going with that Teddy Boy
in the long grass of the meadows by the river,
married in a dress that didn't fit her,
already showing …four months gone –
next seen pushing a pram

another on the way, but what a good mother she is,
everyone singing the Doris Day song '*Que Sera Sera.*'

Your mate pointing at *johnnies* with a stick
in wartime Nissen huts,
creamy yellow or pink, slimy as slugs
or those stranded jellyfish you saw on
Co-op steam train trips to the seaside,
never quite understanding what they were for,
but knew they were maybe to do with sex,
Pat Boone crooning '*Love Letters in the Sand*'.

The girl at school you were secretly in love with,
whose house you rode by every night,
frightened in case she saw you, of not knowing what to
    say or do,
somehow related to those dreams you had,
when you woke to something sticky
as school dinner custard on your pyjama legs,
afterwards ashamed by stains on sheets.

You overheard someone say to your Dad, *she's going
    through the change,*
saw their sympathetic knowing smiles,
and wondered if that's what was happening to you,
    even in your sleep.

The Love Games of Buzzards

Two buzzards draw circles
trying to make the perfect O,
each one tighter
than the last,
sky writing their language of love
until they close the circle,
grappling
one upside down beneath the other,
tangling their talons,
knotting tenderly,
then like twine unspooling,
falling towards the valley's green sheets,
all the time
their shrill mewling protests
neither would ever
hurt the other,
before beginning their gradual drift away.

O, how love snags your heart with its claws,
leaves you speaking the language of empty pillows.

Graphology

For Jean

1

Even without meeting
I would have known you for what you are -
as if you'd stepped out of a page of one of your letters,
a self-portrait
hand-written in your heart's ink,
your honest open loops,
those upright slopes, the strength of each stroke,
the pressure firm, balanced, unambiguous,
every letter generous, rounded out, your O as clearly defined
as a stone, stubborn in a stream,
shaped to withstand the current -
the way nothing hides between your words,
each inhabiting its own space
in a warm geography,
not just lines
but a map to your landscape.

You rolled your hands in ink,
left your hand prints all over my wall.

2

She always said his writing was like a crab
peering out of a hole, waiting to pounce,
a spider fallen into ink
scuttling across a page, trying not to be seen
for what it really is.

Never strictly between the lines, it wanders off,
changes slope, size and character to suit circumstances –
or who it thinks the reader is.
A constant evasion, a book half open,
more a slithering of letters along a line,
knowing how useful full stops are.

Now he sends emails, changes font, cuts and pastes -
relieved to be freed from judgement.

All That Jazz

After 'A Love Supreme' by Ashley Kahn

Lightly fingering keys in anticipation,
they get down to it, straight into
one of those old standards they reach for
as they start their set -
Someday my prince will come, Night and day,
All or nothing at all -
laying down the chords, playing off the melody,
each seeking their own riffs -
wringing out every possibility from songs as familiar
as their own bodies;
getting on those rhythms,
sometimes calling a different time,
sometimes holding back, not going all out, slowing down,
before the drummer hits the high-hat, accents on a snare rim,
or a subtly quicker cymbal ride signals double time,
gooses the rhythm
as the bass double-stops the line, and they move into a blues
set in the minor key, *all smoke and pleasure from pain,*
a voicing in fourths,
each line crests and resolves, exploring the limits,
stretching out time, becomes *Chasin' the Trane*
and the tenor sax touches *that deep dark moan,*
all tension seeking harmonic relief,
long notes played legato flowing into one another –
a crying out in tongues,
those *small soul sermons* we sing in unison
as we come
to the end
touching down again on the tune,
those last overtones, and afterwards
the dying refrain of
What is this thing called love?

Joinery

After months of trying to make you,
and nothing worked,
we took up carpentry, studied the art of making joints,
how the tenon is cut to fit the mortise hole,
has shoulders that form
the seat,
when the joint fully enters,
may be glued,
or pinned
to lock it in place.

We practised the wedged half-dovetail,
the hammer-headed tenon,
the open and through mortise,
how to form the tenon joint when the shoulders cannot be
    tightened with a clamp -

until that night we made you,
when your mother took me by the hand, lead me through
    the downstairs bedroom door,
afterwards
tamping the hand-cut tenon joint,
making sure
everything was pinned in properly.

Let's make another I said, when we were on holiday in Wales,
and we hammered the joint home,
a first time fit,
without even waking your sister
asleep
in her cot beside us.

Changing Geographies

(Wikipedia – 'Continental drift is the movement of the Earth's continents relative to each other by appearing to drift across the ocean bed')

Sometimes we are continents slipping apart,
one from the other,
slowly shifting on the maps
we make of who we are together,
the way America came away
from Africa and Europe.

Other nights we are Gondwana,
every Southern Hemispheric land mass indivisible,
Australia tucked in heel and toe,
spooning with all the rest,
a bodily and emotional congruence -

until the always fluid substrata begin
their pull and tug,
and we drift away,
oceans apart once more.

Millennia later,
we re-inhabit the centre of our oceanic bed,
one body of land slides under the other,
that grinding of tectonic plates as we come together,
exploring those softer topographies mapped out on skin,
the spaces between eyes and thighs, the ridge lines of
    neck and spine,
our continents quietly colliding, riding into one another,
hip to hip,
become a single land again.

Nightfishing for Sea Trout

1

For weeks now the river has been sun–bleached stones
threaded by water,
a slow silence, just maintaining
some kind of flow,
and fish, if there at all, go stale in deeper, darker pools,
hiding their poetry.

Most await the rain, shoaled up off the estuary mouth,
impatient for the faintest taint of fresh water,
their lives on standby.
Only an occasional air-flung flash reveals
a hint of what might be there.

Nothing moves.
How long is it since he took out his rods
and felt the loop and sing
of the line, as it bends and stretches the rod's tip, when he
casts at the water's elusive message?
With little else to do
he sits in the garden untangling line knot by knot,
as if he were unpicking the lock of half-heard sound in his head.

2

Then the weather breaks,
the pressure drops, rain feeds the river.
It colours, surges, then clears.
Sea trout run hard without stopping, all scaled, silvered
muscle aimed at the spawning beds.

At night as the flood recedes,
he slips into the water, false casting, terrified
of foul-hooking himself, of losing his footing, drowning
in the exhilaration of the splash and crash of rising fish.
This is a nightfishing,
where a cast is made into silence
and there is the sudden pull of a mouth-hooked fish
freshly run
on new water.

Blue Sky Thinking

Up on the Vallum ditch, high above Stagshaw Bank,
the view is so clear you think you can see the sea.

Clouds are signatures practised on a blank blue sheet.
Only the valley bottom hides its secrets, tucked under a
    blanket of mist.

It's one of those days for walking hand in hand with what
    you think,
when the sky wears its heart on its sleeve, and you listen

to the steady click as you pace each step with your stick,
sounding out the cut-glass air.

Over to the left, the television mast of Pontop Pike
is broadcasting in high definition -

that sharper vision you wish you had, the delineation
between how things seem and what they are.

Power lines link arms over the landscape
trying to salvage daydreams

with their stilted symmetry, the hum and rattle of electricity
splitting the wind's infinitive,

scoring a line through
what cannot be said out loud.

Anything else is the sound of water,
the earth being wrung out like a dishcloth -

as if you could wring out of yourself
what you cannot yet write.

A blackbird, or is it a thrush,
is remembering how to sing, responding to early warmth,

encouragement that it might be Spring,
the year's false start.

Before you, a field painted with tears of heavy dew
and the footprints of someone else, heading towards
    St. Oswald's Hill;

then the endless dragging sog and suck of paths
lost in mud, and everywhere is a detour from where you
    want to be –

the only way ahead the deer track you follow, down
    through the shadows of trees,
coming out at last to find the sun,

and those blue skies caught in the arms of the Tyne
nosing its way to a clear sight of the sea.

The Day My Mother Met Princess Di

she'd had her hair permed, blue rinsed,
that silvery sheen she thought suited her age,

wore her pale lilac half-sleeved cardy,
one of her floral dresses,

never stopped smiling, hardly
said a cross word all day long.

The picture we have of the Event has her seated
in the wheelchair she had taken to,

like the bloody Queen of Sheba, my Dad said,
as he pushed her around the corridors.

Di is leaning forward, almost bowing
as if offering fealty, shaking Mum's daintily proffered hand,

flashing that smile, eyes as blue as
her massive sapphire and diamond engagement ring.

Mum is lapping up the attention,
pursing her lips, that way she had

when putting on her posh voice,
used like crockery she kept for *best*.

All her life she'd talked in awe of Gracie Fields,
Garbo, Taylor, Hepburn,

that screen royalty she'd seen in films,
or oohed and aahed or tutted about in the Sunday Mirror,

and now, in front of her, shaking her hand,
a real princess, talking to her as if she mattered.

A day she never forgot,
even on days when forgetting was all she did,

her eyes sparking star-bright in a night sky
suddenly cleared of clouds,

a memory as hard as diamonds
clustered round a sapphire void.

Reciting the Alphabet Backwards

At the end
she never left the house,
always closed the curtains to keep the neighbours out,
hid her money in plastic bags,
washed her dishcloths twice a day,
could sing every word of *Danny Boy*.

It was sometimes a puzzle to her to understand quite
    where she was.
She remembered Belfast streets – the Ormeau Road,
the Ravenhill Road, Ballarat Street
as if she'd never left;
spoke to Blodwyn, her childhood friend,
still in the room,
not fifty years of distance and the Irish Sea between,

and then would recite the alphabet backwards,
arriving at A -

forgetting who you were,
at the end.

A Better Man

One day,
shoving barrowed muck up a slope,
he buckled, felled by blood, a slip he said,
shrugged off as if it were nothing,
and no, he wouldn't see the doctor.

At eighty one he still had a quiet strength,
a better man than me,
arms all gaunt muscle,
taut strung bows
shifting forever stuck screws, hoisting weights
beyond my lift or pull -
a knowing, applied like science,
the just when and how to of
real knowledge.

On his last visit
he spent all day lopping trees,
chain sawing logs, feeding the gape of a shredder
while I watched or ran and fetched.
He'd spent his life grafting,
work his grip on pride.

He thought me soft, no use at things that mattered,
possessing all the skills
I never had or managed.
He turned wood, made things work, like he made pastry,
by touch and feel and rub -
not measured, gauged or weighed,
just knowing.
His words were few, garnered for when to use,
like his strength.
I had the words,
but not the knowing.

In the end two more sly, unseen sucker blows
stole the feet from under him,
shunted him into a chair -
that and his deafness shut him almost into silence.
Infection did the rest.
The last of his strength and rattled breath
he kept, eked out - only surrendered
when he knew
we had left the room.

South

*'I want to go south where there is no autumn, where the cold
doesn't crouch over me like a snow-leopard waiting to pounce.'*
D.H. Lawrence letter 3/10/24

All day
the creak and groan,
then the slow thunder of an iceberg calving,
old ice run its course,
sick to death of carrying the drawn-out freight of years,
those accumulations of thousands of days and nights of snow,
layer upon layer folded
under memories of rain and rock
and what was once air, the end-game
of a glacier finished with
sculpting a landscape, grinding out its life,
now giving itself to the sea,
the taste of age and salt,
going
south.

How Bees Survive Winter

1

Triggered by the signal of October's half lit sun -
its one bar fire more seen than felt,

worker bees pin down the drones,
carve off their wings,

as if they were dismantling over-aged,
redundant planes, how you become less

than the sum of your parts,
as your joints pack up, cause you grief at night.

2

Having sawn off their wings,
they bulldoze them over the edge of the lighting board,

a dark cargo slung from a slave-ship on the wrack of a storm,
or drag them inside the hive, shove them to the outer wall,

let them starve, too big a burden
for winter's workhouse fare.

3

Virgin queens no longer fly to mate,
have no need for the suicide flights of drones,

that pact they make: sperm exchanged for
scatterings of bodies from the bee-chased air.

4

This is the time of giving up the game of having it all,
for living off honey stored in the hive,

and what remains
of hope.

Skin

In the mirror
that morning he caught sight of the skin
around his neck jowling,
drooping,
a turkey's naked wattle, all folds and crinkled crests,
and the skin on back of his hands,
wrinkling when pushed, like slowly setting jam
or the silt and sand on a sea bed
stippled into slackening waves.

Blotches of liver spots are freckles gone wrong,
the colour of a newly creosoted fence –
or something worse
perhaps.

Veins stand out like branches of dead ivy
stretched over a brick wall,
skeletal fingers going nowhere.

Once he had skin as supple as his grandson's cheek,
as soft as the softest calfskin glove.
Now it is the shell he wears
hardening like his own history.

Noises Off

The sound of African Kora music sieves our garden air,
    trying to distil
fractured noise into silence -

the buzz of by-pass traffic, the rattle of a local train,
hedge trimmers whining on then off,

whispers of leaves
brushed by afternoon breeze,

murmured
love-yous of pigeons perched on near-by roofs.

A house alarm disturbs the heat haze,
what you think is peace.

A just-fledged magpie grates out its feed-me cackle.

Somewhere piano sonatas are practised badly.

One down, a joiner drills and saws,
discusses joints, Messi's latest goals, the price of vans.

A car passes leaking hip hop
or is it house?

Nearby, chased children shriek, almost drowning out the click
of croquet balls, your neighbour's explanations of the game,
its rules.

Next door, a man dying in a downstairs room,
wonders why sound is so distant,

as if someone
is trying to turn it off.

Getting Ready

Finding your suits, you ponder
which to wear - blue with showy stripes,
or perhaps just plain shadow-dark?

Eventually your black tie emerged from hiding,
with the white shirt you have to iron,
wondering if it was a christening when it was last worn,

as you choose the colour of socks to wear
with those black shoes with the loose heel
that you should have had repaired.

Radio Three plays
the slow, sad movement
of Handel's organ concerto in F major.

What to take? Glasses to read the hymns,
Gibson's ode " Northumberland",
(he was a Redesdale lad born and bred),

coins for the collection,
or should it be notes?
Something to read while you wait – maybe not.

You walk in the garden,
remembering when you saw him last, barely standing,
on two sticks pointing out what to prune.

How like your father he was,
everything done just so, how straight and deep
his double digging, nothing fudged, no complaining.

"You just have to get on with it"
they both always said when asked.
Eventually they both did – after a long dying.

You leave the house for the church,
locking the doors, closing all the windows,
turn your phone to silent.

Blowing Out the Candles

Make a wish Grandad. Make a wish
she screeched, lighting the candles
on the cake she'd teetered on a chair to mix,
licking the spoon as she stirred.

Seven years old, she wishes
to become a princess, a fairy
with wings and a wand,
life still about the next moment,

dressing her latest Barbie, wanting
to make her brother play at schools,
tomorrow
to arrive today.

I blow out the candles,
calculating the algebra
of how long, what's left,
the singularity of one,
(alone).
Today I'm sixty seven,
tomorrows are simple subtractions -
how hard it is to wave a wand for anything

but the relief of another fragile spring,
the garden's tentative greening,
the sight of the sparrow hawk ghosting away
empty handed.

Separate Lives

Side by side they lie,
fingers stroking touch screens,
scrolling separate on-line lives

at angles to each other,
neither a witness to the other's connections,
their various cyber souls,

checking Facebook pages,
the latest count of friends,
their only solace browsing other lives,

how their postings tick up likes,
each other
a third person reference

in all their texts and tweets.
They apologise, if the toes of a foot by chance
grazes the other's softest skin just behind the knee,

the way a broadband signal
sometimes buffers, flickers
and then disappears.

Schrödinger's Cat

sits haunched
outside the window rolling its rrs,
stares in,
eyes brimful saucers, pupils
contracting and dilating like lenses
on a closed - circuit television camera, tracking

their every move, ears pricked, listening to their lives
as they watch the evening news,
the report of a disabled man mugged,
the latest cure for cancer,
ignore the fifth cold - call of the day
selling solar panels, while she

stirs the stew she says is tagine, asking for a glass
of wine to be poured,
Go on, it's not a fasting day -
indulging in the usual winge about the washing up,
the failure to sort the car insurance,
to phone the solicitor
to revise their wills – whose fault it is.

The cat scratches an ear, licks the fur on its paw,
contemplates the theory of quantum superposition,
drifts through walls,
through rooms ravelled in stubborn silence,
those countless combinations of
alternative marital universes

collapsing one into another, as they re-imagine
the magic of touch, him stroking
the slack soft skin of eye lids, the pit of her back,

Rub my temple, my neck she asks -
how they hold hands watching a film, fall asleep,
    shoulder resting on shoulder,
tip toe around each others' dreams,
avoid the word alone,

all these indeterminate worlds
folded like paper within their walls,
more unseen than seen –
how to be both,
how to be it all.

Cliff Walking

'We are the song death takes its time singing' Robert Hass

Here at Weybourne the land is swallowing itself
                                        slowly,
        the very thought stuck in its throat,
                before being washed down at last by the sea,
unheld, like a heart
                        missing a beat,
    set to the music of skylarks
                            rising and
            falling away on the air of their own songs,
                                the way these cliffs
        ape the shape of the waves,

                                            all peaks

                and troughs
unanchored by their own
                    downward momentum,
                            crests waiting to be unknitted,
as the sea rewinds its clock
                    and unwinds earth,
                            waves wagging their tongues,
    whispering *what if, what if.*

There is no firm ground.   Life is
a slow puncture   air escaping unseen   bit by bit.

On the news today,
    Michelangelo's David is crumbling from within,
        the way the body's art is grounded in imperfection,
gradually failing,
        how a badly-hung door swings loosely on its hinges,
                                            opens
    then closes.

You think you know what's happening -
                    that pain, a dull bruise in your chest rises
and recedes -
                    but keep on anyway, staying the path,
watching the skylarks
            climbing the stairs of the sky,
                        hanging onto the air, hearing them sing
time is selfish, selfish, selfish.

Walking the Ridgeline

To be here at last, catching your breath
from crossing the ridge,
poised between one valley and another,

watching the sun fall under the horizon's blanket,
while the wind sheers and veers to North
carving age into your face like a blade on ice.

Landmarks are indistinct --
symbols on the map of the journey here,
the way you catch the flash in the darkening

down there in the distance,
the sign of something coming,
or going,

as headlights turn a corner,
and you hear the mistle thrush singing premonitions
of night.

Is this ridgeline
just words and the sky pouring off
the edge of the horizon?

The smudge of smoke from dying hillside heather fires?
The faint hum of car wheels
on a failing road?

Or the shadows of leafless trees,
at that border between field and forest,
creeping closer?

Perhaps it's time to come down off the hill,
close the curtains on this dark, keep the heat in,
lay the fire, hope for warmth -

give up counting days,
or breaths,
one by one.

Bird Notes

1) Open

The small epiphanies of blackcaps singing
meaning to themselves, lost
inside the smirr of morning mist;

a firecrest tugging out the strings of guts from moth larvae -
as if it were examining the tangled entrails
of its own life;

the dipper's bib pulses white
through the sepia wash of peat-inked water,
pursuing the river's soul;

the way you walk bare-headed in the rain
relishing wetness, your uncovered heart turned inside out
still open to it all.

2) A Sudden Hawk

coming out of nothing,
silent as air,
a life in hold
and then,
a shroud of feathers
shifts in the wind
like a shadow
on a lung –
everything in balance
as it plucks at flesh, perched on the fence
oblivious.

Robin Moss

Robin Moss was born and brought up in Suffolk, before leaving for further education at the University of Sussex and the London School of Economics. He has lived in the North East for over forty years, and worked as a full time Trade Union Officer before his retirement. He is married and has two daughters and four grandchildren. He has written poetry since his late teens, and more seriously since his retirement. At school he was introduced by a wonderful English teacher to the poetry of Yeats, Hughes, Gunn, Plath and the war poets, and was heavily influenced by the folk poetry of Bob Dylan and the rock poetry of Chuck Berry. He has always read extensively especially poetry, even when not writing. This is a first publication apart from four poems published in Pending Poetry in 2014, one of which is included here, "A Better Man".